Much Ado About Something Else

Written by Andrew Smith

Pathfinders

Contents

Page	
3	Programme Notes
4	All the World's a Youth Group!
8	Counting Sand ... God knows what he's doing
10	The Job Briefing ... Honouring God's name
12	The Sheep Stuffer's Sentence ... Justice
14	This Thing Called Love ... God's idea of love
16	A Likely Story ... God of the details
18	Veronica's Virulent Virus ... Being saved
20	It's Happened! ... Spreading the good news
22	One Man and his Voice ... The Good Shepherd
24	United ... The peace of God
26	The Court Case ... Hypocrisy
28	Ananias, Where Are You? ... Obedience
30	Conversation Pieces ... Witnessing
32	The Soap Superstar ... Help from the Holy Spirit
34	The Perfect Sculpture ... What will we be like in heaven?
36	Manic Mike's Paranoia Problem ... Self-control
38	You've Been Warned! ... Jesus' return
40	To Work or Not to Work ... Preparing for Jesus' return
42	The Challenge ... Temptation
44	The Pat Rowaneyes Show ... Belief and action
46	Too Good To Be True ... Recognizing the enemy
48	Bible index

Programme Notes

Eleven to fourteen year olds often fall between a church's children's group and its youth group, but they need resources and activities to suit them, so that they can learn about God and grow in their Christian lives. Young teenagers like things that happen, things that are entertaining and things that involve the leaders getting water thrown at them!

First *Much Ado About Something* and now *Much Ado About Something Else* contain all this and more, with twenty tried and tested sketches each, and practical guidelines for using drama with this age group. Some sketches are funny, a few are serious-ish, most are fairly silly. But they all help teach the Bible to young teenagers and will challenge them about their relationship with God.

The sketches will work in a variety of settings – a weekly group, a family service, a mission or a school assembly. They're all easy to learn, not-too-hard to do, and short. They could all be performed equally well by leaders, or by members of the group who see themselves as budding actors.

DIRECTOR'S TIPS

These will help you understand what crazy ideas I had in mind when I wrote the sketch. They also give you hints and tips on how to perform it to the best of your ability.

Throughout the book I have referred to 'performers', 'audiences' and 'stages'. Don't worry, I'm not expecting you to hire the local theatre and put on an evening's entertainment of Pathfinder sketches – although it would be great if you did! Anyone playing any of the parts in any sketch counts as a 'performer', anyone watching counts as 'audience', and wherever you do the sketch counts as a 'stage'. I know it sounds all very dramatic and grand, but I had to call them something and 'performer', 'audience' and 'stage' seemed as good as anything!

Many of the sketches in *Much Ado About Something Else* have come from other Pathfinder resources. Since they were first published, some have been rewritten to make them even better than they were originally. I hope it has worked!

TRAILER

If you want to perform the sketches on their own, or a number of them at one event, each comes with a 'trailer'. This is a short sentence you can use after the sketch to help the young people think about the issues raised.

WORKSHOP

These suggestions will help you use the sketch in a group session. They include a discussion starter, where appropriate, and exploration of the relevant Bible verses. Many of the sketches were originally written to fit in with a specific theme for a group session. This has been reflected in the titles and workshop explanations. However, if you think you can teach another point just as well from the sketch, go ahead. Use them how, when and where you like.

All the World's a Youth Group!

Using drama with 11-14s

Your idea of drama with young teenagers might begin and end with getting them to act out the Parable of the Good Samaritan. There's nothing wrong with that, but drama needn't stop there – or start there, for that matter! With time and effort, it can become a valuable and exciting part of your group's life together, with relationships strengthened, issues aired, questions raised, and the Bible explored in dynamic, new ways.

The two basic reasons for doing drama with your group are

1. Someone has asked you to perform a sketch in the family service in two weeks' time and you're panicking
2. You want to use drama to help your group explore for themselves what God is saying in the Bible.

Whichever reason you start with, remember...

The golden rules

- Tell whoever has asked you to perform the sketch that you normally need at least four weeks' notice, if you're going to do it well.
- You and your group need to work thoroughly at the part of the Bible you want to use as a basis for drama.
- Drama takes time – the more time you put into it the more your group members will get out of it.
- Get everyone used to drama by having some group sessions where all the activities are drama-based. This will help you spot those who are keen on drama and those who are good at it.
- Consider running a separate drama group for those who want to do it. In any group there'll always be some who don't like drama – they could be very embarrassed and discouraged if it became a major item every week.

1. Drama for performance

However many brilliant drama books (like this one!) are published, you'll eventually come across part of the Bible about which a sketch has never been written. So the only thing to do is to create your own. The two basic ways of creating a sketch are

- to **improvise** it (make it up) with your group
- to **write** a script from your own imagination.

Improvisation

Work hard on the Bible verses yourself, using commentaries, map books, Bible handbooks, concordances and other helps. Get 'under the skin' of what God is saying.

Give the potential performers of the sketch a starting-point based on the verses. Then, to begin with at least, give them space to go where they like with it. For example, suppose you wanted a sketch about David and Goliath, and have decided to focus on David's discussions with his brothers. You might set it up with your performers like this...

'Simon, you play David. You saw Goliath laugh at the Israelites and it made you mad. You're young and angry. Julie and Peter, you're David's brothers – battle-hardened soldiers who know that no one can beat Goliath. You think David is just a young, foolish kid, but you feel responsible for him. David, you're telling your brothers of your plan to fight Goliath. Brothers, react to what David is saying. You can end it anyway you want to.'

When they have finished, talk about how it went – the good bits and the bits that didn't really work.

Now that they have improvised what they *think* might have happened, look at the Bible verses together and discover what *did* actually happen.

Get them to run through it again, remembering the good bits and trying to find new ways of playing the others. Encourage them to incorporate any changes they need to make as a result of examining the Bible verses for themselves, and also anything you yourself have discovered in your own study.

After a couple more run-throughs, write down a basic version of the plot that you all agree on.

Now run it again, encouraging the group to use the same lines each time and to try to remember them. You may not need to write all the lines out word for word – the performers will have probably learnt them by this stage.

Keep rehearsing right up to the big day so that your performers eventually reproduce their work effortlessly… well, you know what I mean!

Writing

As before, always start with the Bible verses. Make sure you understand what God is saying through them and therefore what point you want to communicate through your sketch.

Getting started is often the hardest part. Look for inspiration from props that a character might use and from other sketches or situations that might lend themselves to the point you're trying to make.

Always remember that you're trying to tell a story. Even the shortest sketch should have a beginning, a middle and an end. The audience needs to know *who* the characters are, *where* they are and *what's* happening.

As you work on the sketch, keep referring back to the Bible verses to check you're still being true to their message.

Think of the characters in the sketch as real people. Decide if they're clever, easily bored, mature, selfish or whatever. Keep them consistent throughout the sketch, reacting in their own particular way to different events.

Think back to the moods and emotions that you find in the Bible verses. Is there an underlying tension? Are the characters afraid, excited or joyful? The Bible might not say all this explicitly, but often the narrative will imply it.

Get other people to critique your sketch. Make sure they can work out what's going on. It's easy for *you* to understand, but someone else might struggle to follow your train of thought. Ask them to be honest about the clarity of your message, the jokes and the plot.

What 'soaks in' when you do drama

Using drama in any form can teach both explicitly and implicitly. This book is full of explicit teaching through sketches, but as your group members get involved in drama, they'll learn a lot of good things implicitly, like…

- to trust each other
- not to laugh at each other when they make mistakes
- to be trustworthy by not letting down their fellow performers
- team work
- mutual encouragement
- how to face and handle failure.

Look for ways of highlighting these implicit lessons as you notice them being learnt during your drama.

2. *Drama for teaching*

Here are a few ways of getting 'under the skin' of different parts of the Bible using drama.

Group improvisations

Use the kind of Bible-based situation suggested above for David and his brothers, but instead of only one group of performers, have several smaller groups working at once. Young people who find drama difficult will feel more comfortable like this. If everyone else is acting in their own improvisations, they'll know they're not being watched. Go round all the groups and talk to them about their work. Ask them how they're getting on, feed in suggestions and encourage them. At the end of the allotted time, don't feel you have to get everyone watching every small group's improvisation.

As well as Bible-based situations, try setting up issues or predicaments relevant to your group members, e.g. being pressured to take drugs or being challenged about their faith. Always encourage group members to try out improvisations rather than plan them. This releases greater honesty and naturalness about the situations.

When the group becomes more experienced, you could interview group members in character, for instance as Goliath just before his fight with David, or as Peter just after Pentecost.

Directed improvisations

This might sound like a contradiction, but it can actually help groups that aren't used to drama to explore big stories or issues.

Have a rough idea of what the improvisation is about and where it's going to go. Feed in your suggestions to the whole group. Encourage them to act to your suggestions, all the time adding their own ideas. You need to react to their ideas and build on their new observations.

A directed improvisation about Noah might go something like this...

'I want you all to imagine that Simon here is Noah and he has told you all about God's plan for the ark. You are all his family. Noah, you've got to persuade everyone to help you. As Noah gets to you, imagine how you'd feel if your dad told you to help build a huge boat. Off you go, Noah. *(Allow a couple of minutes for Noah to try to persuade people.)*

Now imagine it's a few days later and Noah has finally persuaded you to help build the boat, but there's not much time left. This half of the group, use anything you can find to build an ark we can all fit into. The rest, start rounding up all the animals.

Sarah, you check that they have all arrived. Noah, make sure the boat is built correctly. Don't waste time – the rain will be here any minute now! Sarah, make sure the lions are kept separate from the sheep. Peter, can you make sure the snakes are secure? Is the ark nearly finished? Harry is bringing in the elephants – quick, find room for them!

Now it's time for everyone to get into the ark – make sure there's room for you! But what about your friends outside? How do you feel about them? What are you going to do for them? God has shut the door, so now there's no way out. I should try and get comfy – you're going to be in there for a long time. Has anyone seen the spiders? Or the rats? The boat's beginning to float now. That must mean the water is really deep. What do you think has happened to your friends who aren't in the ark? How do you feel now? Show me with your bodies as well as your faces how you're feeling...', and so on.

Sample Drama Session

Spreading the Good News

Aim

To help the young people learn that it's important to spread the Good News of Christ by both our words and our actions

Warm-up

Play a couple of running-around games to get everyone going and lively. 'Budge' was always a favourite with my group. It's basically 'Tig' but with a number of bases. There can only be one person on a base at a time. If someone else wants to get on the base, they say 'Budge!' and the other person has to go. Players can't be caught while they're on a base.

Calming down

Now play a game that helps everyone to calm down ready for work, but that also gets them concentrating and using their imagination.

The 'Shopping Game' is a good one for this. Everyone sits in a circle and, in turn, says their name and something they bought whilst shopping. Each person has to say all the previous items before adding their own.

'Unusual Objects' is another classic. Have as a prop a fairly bland object such as a stick. Each person takes it in turn to mime something that the stick could be, e.g. a snooker cue, telescope or giant pen. The rest of the group then guesses what it is. When they have guessed, the prop is passed on to the next person.

The rest of the session will consist of three role-plays which the young people do in small groups.

Market stalls

Have a good supply of different household objects. Anything will do. Slightly more obscure items work better, like a sink plunger or a scouring pad. Give each person one of them. Say that they have one minute to think of a use for that object which isn't its normal use. When they have thought of something, put them into pairs and tell them that one of them has to try to sell their object to the other person by convincing them of how brilliant their object is. Allow two minutes for them to do this, then swap over.

Look at **1 Thessalonians 2:1-12**. Paul recounts his work of spreading the gospel to the church at Thessalonica. Verse 9 tells us he worked hard at it because he knew it was something good to pass on. He was like the seller in the improvisation – a person with something he or she longed for others to have. Our desire to tell others about Jesus should match the excitement generated in trying to sell the object, not that our job is to 'sell' Jesus.

Getting the message

In pairs, set up the following improvisation. A is a Director of Science at a leading university, responsible for the whole department and its budget. B is a scientist obsessed with UFOs – which A finds very irritating. A doesn't believe in UFOs. Last night a UFO landed in B's back garden. B has now gone to A to try to get £250,000 for research into this UFO. The aliens refuse to come to the university or allow B to take anything from the UFO. The scene starts with B knocking on A's door.

Don't give the pairs any time to prepare – they have to start the improvisation immediately.

Afterwards, talk about the improvisations. Who managed to get the money? Who thought B had gone loopy? Ask the people playing B what could have made it easier for them to get the money. Draw out the point that, if they could have thought about it properly and prepared a good speech, they would have stood a better chance of getting the money.

Verse 8 shows that Paul spent a lot of time telling people about Jesus. He knew what to say, unlike B. Give each person a piece of paper with two speech bubbles on. In the first they should write their description of a Christian and in the second how they became a Christian. If there are some in the group who aren't Christians, ask them to write why they come along.

The car crash

Set up this improvisation in groups of four. A is a pedestrian, B is a car driver, C is another pedestrian and D is an ambulance driver. A is walking across a zebra crossing when B drives along and knocks him or her over. C sees all this happen. The performers decide what happens next. They can call for help, rob the person who has been knocked over, beat up the driver – anything! But throughout the improvisation the only word anyone can say is 'waffle'. Again, don't give them time to prepare.

Afterwards, discuss how well each person understood what was going on in their group. Did they understand the other characters? How were they able to communicate? Draw out that it was through their actions and reactions that they could communicate. They didn't need to say anything for other people to know what they meant.

Look at verses 6 to12. Paul, Silas and Timothy didn't just talk to the people in Thessalonica, they showed them what it was like to be a Christian. If we're to be effective witnesses, we must communicate the Good News through both our words and our actions.

Get the groups to think about how they could live differently so that their actions as well as their words speak clearly to their friends.

Pray for opportunities to talk about Jesus, for courage to live for him and for his strength to do all this.

Counting Sand

ABRAHAM Very old but very wise
MURDOCH Their cynical servant

(MURDOCH looks around anxiously. ABRAHAM staggers past with a pile of towels.)

MURDOCH: *(To the audience)* Poor old Abraham. He really believes Sarah's going to have a baby! Says God told them or something. Whoever heard of someone over ninety having a baby? *(ABRAHAM hurries past. MURDOCH calls after him.)* Still no news? *(To the audience)* Probably just a bad case of wind. *(ABRAHAM dashes back with more towels and a bowl of water.)* It'll be heartbreaking when they find out.

ABRAHAM: *(Entering very excitedly)* It's a boy! God's given us a beautiful baby boy! We're going to call him Isaac.

M: She's *really* had a baby?

A: Of course! What do you *think* she had – a bad case of wind?

M: Errmmm...

A: Well, don't just stand there – start counting the sand. God promised us as many descendants as grains of sand on the shore and stars in the sky. Go on, we need to know how many birthday cards to buy. *(ABRAHAM exits.)*

M: Count the sand? This is going to take years! *(He picks up some sand and starts to count the grains out loud. Someone walks across carrying a sign saying 'A Few Years Later'. MURDOCH counts silently for a few seconds, then starts counting out loud.)* Forty million eight hundred thousand and fifty-four, forty million eight hundred thousand and fifty-five, forty million eight hundred thousand and fifty-six... *(He carries on counting silently.)*

A: *(ABRAHAM enters in a state of panic.)* Murdoch! Murdoch? *(He nudges MURDOCH, making him spill the sand.)*

M: Forty million eight hundred thousand and sixty... Aaaaarrrggghhh! Now look what you've done! I'll have to start all over again!

A: Don't worry about that. We've got more important things to do. God's told me to take Isaac away and kill him.

M: *(Not fully realizing)* That's nice... *(Realizing)* What? You can't do that!

A: Why not?

M: Well, it will hurt for one thing. And anyway, how will you ever have millions of descendants if you kill Isaac?

A: God will sort it out.

M: I'd like to see him try!

A: *Would* you? Then we'll leave tomorrow... *(Suddenly sad)* And, Murdoch... don't forget to sharpen my big knife. *(ABRAHAM starts to leave. MURDOCH goes back to counting the sand silently. ABRAHAM notices and calls back.)* Oh, and Murdoch? *(MURDOCH looks up.)* I think this means you can stop doing that now. *(ABRAHAM exits sadly.)*

M: *(Leaping into the air with joy)* Yes! *(Starts singing)* Oh, I don't like to be beside the seaside, Oh, I don't like to be beside the sea... *(He exits to fetch a sign saying 'A Few Days Later'. He brings it back on and dances around with it, still singing.)*

A: *(ABRAHAM enters excitedly.)* Murdoch! Murdoch? *(ABRAHAM tries to communicate with MURDOCH who's still singing and dancing around.)* Listen, it's just struck me. God *did* sort it out. There on the mountain he told me not to hurt Isaac, right? He said, 'It's OK. Now I *know* you fear me because you haven't kept back your only son.' And he provided a ram for us to kill instead, remember?

M: *(Still singing and dancing)* Yeah, yeah.

A: Well, Murdoch, you know what all this *means*, don't you?

M: A luxury cruise down the Nile? A three-month party? A teensy-weensy feast at least?

A: *(Ecstatically happy)* No, much better than that – you can start counting the sand again!

M: *(Stopped dead in his tracks)* Uhhh! *(They both freeze.)*

© CPAS 1996

God Knows What He's Doing

DIRECTOR'S TIPS

Throughout, the performers need to maintain a balance between the humour of Murdoch and the seriousness of the sacrifice.

Whoever plays Murdoch will need to be confident at singing and dancing or at least at making a fool of him/herself.

Abraham should be physically very old and frail, but mentally alert.

Have a small amount of sand lying around for Murdoch to count.

TRAILER

When everything seems out of control, who's really in charge?

WORKSHOP

Divide everyone into pairs or small groups. Give each pair or small group a sheet drawn to look like a diary, with four days represented. Ask the groups to look up the following sets of Bible verses and, for each, fill in one day of the diary as if they're Abraham. Get them to try to express his feelings about what has actually happened, but they should keep the diary entries very short.

Genesis 17:15-19
Genesis 21:1-7
Genesis 22:1-2
Genesis 22:12-14

Abraham must have experienced a whole range of emotions during this time – excitement, confusion, amazement, fear, unhappiness – but he knew that God would be faithful to his word. Again in small groups, discuss times when our emotions change. Encourage everyone to be honest enough to say what they sometimes feel about God during these times.

We need to learn to be like Abraham and to trust God in spite of our emotions. He's God and he's *definitely* in control.

The Job Briefing

MRS FED Starting a new job
MRS DUNN A manager briefing MRS FED about her job

(MRS DUNN is sitting at her desk. There's a knock at the door.)

DUNN: Come in. *(MRS FED enters.)*

FED: Good morning, Mrs Dunn. I'm Mrs Fed. I've just started work here.

D: Ah, our new member of staff. Do sit down. Now then, Mrs Fed, it's great to have you on our staff. Has anyone explained your job to you?

F: Not really, no.

D: Right, well, your job will be over Soon.

F: But I've only just started!

D: Pardon?

F: You said my job will be over soon, but I've only just started. I can't be fired yet.

D: No, no. Your job is to supervise our apprentice, young Robin Soon.

F: Oh, I see. I'll be over Soon.

D: That's right, and whilst you're here, you'll be under Payed.

F: I will not! I've signed my contract, and it states that I'll get £200 a week, plus overtime.

D: What *are* you going on about?

F: It's what *you're* going on about that worries me. I can't afford to be underpaid.

D: Will you calm down! I'm not talking about your pay. I'm referring to your boss, Mr Payed.

F: Ah, right! So I'm going to be under Payed, but the job will be over Soon. So where do *you* fit into all this, Mrs Dunn?

D: Me? Oh, I'm over Payed and under Worked.

F: Yes, I can *tell* that.

D: Pardon?

F: Nothing.

D: *(Very suspicious)* Hmmmm... Well, as I was saying, I work over Mr Payed but under Mr Worked.

F: So, in fact, my job here will be under Payed, under Dunn and under Worked, but it will be over Soon.

D: That's it! *Now* you've got the hang of it.

F: So is anybody over Worked?

D: *(Wearily)* Oh, we *all* are.

F: You just said we're all under Worked, but I'd be under Payed as well.

D: Oh, over *Worked*... I see. Yes, just the boss who's a Miss Tree.

F: What? You mean no one knows who it is?

D: No, it's a Miss Tree. If we didn't know who it was, it would be a mystery. *(She doesn't realize what she has just said.)*

F: Well, if you *know* who it is, how can it be a mystery?

D: It's a Miss Tree – Mr Tree's daughter.

F: Oh – Miss Tree, not mystery. Oooh, I see! Right, well, that makes it clear then. While I'm here I'll be under Payed, under Dunn and under Worked. The boss is a Miss Tree, but my job will be over Soon.

D: That's right! You see? It's simple when you know everyone.

F: Well, all I can say is I'm glad I'm not Robin Soon.

D: Why's that, Mrs Fed?

F: Because as well as being under Worked and under Payed, from today he's going to be under Fed as well!

© CPAS 1996

Honouring God's Name

DIRECTOR'S TIPS

> Rehearse the lines very carefully so that the performers get all the names right.

> The performers should listen for groans and laughs, and pause before going on.

> Make sure both characters stand up at different points. Mrs Fed could leap up angrily, whilst Mrs Dunn could walk up and down as she explains the situation.

TRAILER

God said we should honour his name. How do *you* use God's name?

WORKSHOP

Find out the middle names of all the leaders who work with your group, or of other well-known people in the church, school or club. Write each name on a separate sheet of paper and display them all round the room. Give the group five minutes to work out which of the leaders they belong to.

Afterwards, ask the group if any of them would like to tell everyone their middle name. This will almost certainly cause some amusement and possibly embarrassment. Be sensitive about forcing people to give their names if they don't want to. We often find middle names funny because we're not used to thinking of people being called something different.

In the sketch, everyone had a laugh at people's names and the confusion they caused. In Bible times, laughing at someone's name was a great insult to the person and to their family – their name summed up who they were (**Exodus 20:7**). Using God's name as an insult or a joke – or laughing about who he is or giving him less than he deserves – insults him. Jesus said we should *honour* God's name (**Luke 11:2**).

The Sheep Stuffer's Sentence

JUDGE LORD CHIEF JUSTICE BALDYCOOT
HUGH MYRRH Defendant
JURY MEMBER
JURY MEMBERS with no lines to say

	(The scene is a courtroom.)
JUDGE:	I trust the jury has reached a verdict in this most perplexing case?
JURY MEMBER:	Yes, we have, Lord Chief Justice Baldycoot.
J:	Good, then please tell the court – how did the jury find the defendant Mr Hugh Myrrh?
JM:	We just looked in the box and there he was, Lord Chief Justice Baldycoot.
J:	What I meant was, how did you *find* him – guilty or not guilty?
JM:	Oh guilty. Definitely guilty, Lord Chief Justice Baldycoot.
J:	Then it simply remains for me to pass sentence. Before I do so, do you have anything to say, Mr Hugh Myrrh, now that you've been found guilty of these terrible crimes?
HUGH MYRRH:	*(During this speech Hugh becomes increasingly emotional. In the background the tune of* Land of Hope and Glory *is played, starting quietly and getting louder.)* Yes, I would just like to say to those assembled here that I am innocent. I have done nothing wrong, and I believe that one day truth and justice will prevail. A new day will dawn upon society, when the innocent will be released and the guilty punished, when women and children will walk safe and free, when the poor will be made rich and the lonely welcomed, the sick made well and everyone proud to be alive. It will be a brave new era for the world when everyone will...
J:	*(Interrupting, with the music stopping abruptly)* Young man, what *are* you on about?
HM:	I was just stating my innocence and embracing a new and joyful era... *(The music starts again, loudly.)* ...when the lonely will be welcomed, the poor made rich, the guilty punished and the innocent set free, when...
J:	Stop! *(The music stops.)* Thank you. Now don't start all that sentimental rubbish again.
HM:	But I am innocent. I was simply practising the noble art of taxidermy – the science of stuffing animals to preserve them for future generations. *(The music starts again, fairly loudly.)* I wanted to protect a time-honoured tradition which has been passed down from generation to generation and which will benefit our society until that glorious day when the lonely will be welcomed, the poor made rich, the guilty...
J:	Shut up! *(The music stops.)* Will you stop prattling on? And while we've stopped, will *you* (*Addressing the JURY MEMBERS*) go and do something about that awful music? *(The JURY MEMBERS go and deal with the problem in a suitably destructive manner.)* Thank you. As I was saying, the reason that *you* are guilty and thousands of other taxidermists aren't, is that they stuffed *dead* animals. To date you have stuffed *alive* three ferrets, two gerbils, fourteen goldfish, one goat and a flock of spotted sheep. This doesn't include your failed attempts at a maggot and a chihuahua. Neither shall I mention some nasty goings-on with a bull and two tons of straw. You're clearly guilty and I therefore have no option but to impose the heaviest penalty – a fine of £20,000.
HM:	But, but, but...
J:	However, since all your bizarre crimes were committed against animals on my farm, I'm going to... *(He pauses and looks at HUGH MYRRH.)* ...pay the fine myself. You're a free man. What's more, to show that I have forgiven you, you're invited to our house for dinner tonight. We're having chicken... *without* stuffing.

© CPAS 1996

Justice

DIRECTOR'S TIPS

If you can't find Land of Hope and Glory, use something equally stirring.

Practise with the music a few times so that it starts and stops on cue, and is at the right volume.

Don't forget that a pause is where the characters are thinking about what they're doing, not when the performers are trying to remember their lines!

When the judge looks at Hugh at the end, just before he says he'll pay the fine, pause for three seconds while the audience waits for Hugh to be condemned.

TRAILER

The judge paid Hugh's fine. Wouldn't it be great if someone else paid for all our wrongdoings? Well, *Jesus* did.

WORKSHOP

Make a large snakes and ladders board (perhaps on an overhead projector acetate). Divide the group into four teams. Play the game with two dice. The rules are as normal except that, if players slide down a snake, they have to throw a 5 or more to stay in the game. Otherwise they're out because they died of snakebite.

Explore **John 3:14-17**. Jesus was reminding Nicodemus of the incident in **Numbers 21:4-9**. A bronze snake was lifted up on a pole and, when the Israelites who had been bitten by snakes looked at it, God healed them. In the same way, Jesus was lifted up when he was crucified to save people from God's punishment for sin.

Lord Chief Justice Baldycoot was being just when he sentenced Hugh for his criminal offences. But he was also merciful – he not only forgave Hugh but paid the fine as well. Draw out the parallels with God's justice and his mercy, in 'paying the fine' for our sin by sending Jesus to die.

This Thing Called Love

Unfaithfulness

PHIL Ruth's boyfriend
PAUL Ruth's boyfriend
RUTH Phil's and Paul's girlfriend

(RUTH and PHIL are romantically entwined on a seat.)
PHIL: Oh Ruth, I do love you.
RUTH: Oh Paul, you're so scrummy, so warm, so affectionate! I feel so special when I'm with you, with your gorgeous eyes and lovely voice. I *do* love, you hunny-bun. You won't leave me for anyone else, will you? Because I *adore* you, Paul.
PHIL: *(Looking confused)* But I'm *Phil*. *(PAUL enters also looking confused.)* He's Paul.
RUTH: *(Embarrassed)* Ah…

Gossip

SHARON, DAVE, HELEN and **CLIVE** Four friends

(Four friends stand in a row in this order – SHARON, DAVE, HELEN, CLIVE. They face the audience standing perfectly still. When it's their turn to speak, they become animated and then return immediately to being still. Another friend STEVE enters and crosses in front of them all. He stands next to CLIVE. As he passes SHARON she waves, calls 'Hello!' and becomes still again. There's a pause for three seconds.)
SHARON: *(To DAVE)* Hello, Dave. Did you see my mate Steve walk by? I quite like him really.
(There's another three-second pause.)
DAVE: *(To HELEN)* Hello, Helen. Did you see my mate Steve walk by? Don't tell anyone but Sharon really fancies him.
(There's another three-second pause.)
HELEN: *(To CLIVE)* Hello, Clive. Did you see my mate Steve walk by? Don't tell anyone but Sharon's madly in love with him.
(There's another three-second pause.)
CLIVE: *(To STEVE)* Hello, mate. 'Ere, good news about you and Sharon getting engaged!
(All the characters freeze with DAVE and HELEN standing still, CLIVE looking really pleased, and STEVE and SHARON looking shocked.)

Sacrifice

GAIL and **KAY** Two friends

GAIL: Hi, Kay! Do you want the good news or the bad news first?
KAY: Give me the bad news first, thanks, Gail.
G: Well, I could only get one ticket for the Stunners sell-out show on Saturday. It's a real shame 'cos it's gonna be brill! They'll all be there – Steve Stunner, Simon Stunner, Stuart Stunner and of course the dreamiest of them all… Bob. And I'm sure they'll play all their hits – *Since I Saw You, Sue, I've Been in a Stew, Seven Seas Separated Us with Such Sweet Sorrow, Sing a Song of Sixpence*… It'll be a night to remember.
K: Yeah, OK, OK. But you could only get one ticket? So what's the *good* news?
G: *You* can have it.

© CPAS 1996

God's Idea of Love

DIRECTOR'S TIPS

The performers should try not to laugh when they're being romantic. The audience will probably laugh anyway but, if the performers join in, the sketch will die.

The characters in *Gossip* need to practise changing from being a statue to being real. The sharper the change the better it will look.

Make sure the last lines are delivered well. They are the punch lines to the sketch. If people in the audience miss these, they'll miss the point.

Don't be tempted to think that, because these sketches are short, they won't take much effort. They'll need to be learnt and practised just as thoroughly as longer sketches if they're going to be good.

TRAILER

When you say to someone 'I love you', what do you mean?

WORKSHOP

Display the following words – 'sale', 'skip', 'lean', 'stroke', 'pen' and 'stem'. Give the group two minutes to work out a brief definition of each word. Tell them to decide for themselves what the word means.

Then ask them to work out the connection between all these words. Listen to some of the definitions and see if anyone has worked out the connection – all the words have at least two different meanings.

All the sketches were about love, or the lack of love. Ask the group, in pairs, to write a definition of love based on the sketches they have seen. Let them read out their answers if they want to. When we talk about love, we can mean many different things. When Jesus spoke about love, he *knew* what he was talking about.

Look at **John 15:9-13**. Jesus is talking to his disciples about love. In verse 13 he gives us a clear picture of love. Display this verse for the group to see. This is sacrificial love – putting others before ourselves. In the last sketch Gail sacrificed her ticket so that Kay could go to see the Stunners. Jesus sacrificed his life so that we can go to heaven.

A Likely Story

DODGY DAVE The owner of Dave's Donkeys
PHILIP and **BARTHOLOMEW** Two of Jesus' disciples

(The props needed for this sketch are a sign saying 'Dave's Donkeys' and a hobby horse or similar as a 'donkey'. PHILIP and BARTHOLOMEW enter looking around anxiously. They approach the 'donkey' and start to untie it.)

PHILIP: Are you *sure* about this?

BART: Yeah, it's no problem. Leave everything to me.

P: Remember to say who wants it.

B: No, that'll only complicate things. I'll just use my natural charm.

P: But why did we have to come *here*?

B: Because *he* said 'Go and find a donkey', and what better place to find one than at a second-hand donkey dealer's?

P: That's what I *mean*. Getting a donkey from Dodgy Dave is daft. A friend of mine bought one. He'd only got a little way down the road when one of its back legs fell off!

B: You worry too much. Just untie this one, and we'll be off.

(They untie the donkey, acting as if it's alive and struggling. There are cries of 'Whoa, Dobbin!' and similar. DODGY DAVE hears the commotion and enters looking angry.)

DAVE: Can I *help* you?

P: We're just taking this donkey, if that's OK?

D: Well, funnily enough, it's *not* OK. If you want to test ride one, come into the office and we'll sort out the paperwork.

P: *(To BARTHOLOMEW)* I *said* we shouldn't do this.

B: *(To PHILIP)* Shut *up*! *(To DAVE)* Look, we need this donkey for a very important job. It'll only be gone a short time, and I can guarantee it'll be well looked after.

D: *(Very sarcastic)* Oh well, that's alright then. Tell you what – don't just take *that* one, take them all! In fact, why not have the whole business?

P: *(To himself)* We just want one with all four legs, that's all. *(DAVE gives PHILIP a dirty look and BARTHOLOMEW kicks PHILIP.)*

B: *(To PHILIP)* I told you to shut *up*! *(To DAVE)* Now *you're* a reasonable man. We just want to borrow this fine animal for a short while, then we'll return it. It's for a very important occasion. You'll appreciate the need for careful and discreet negotiations.

D: You're right. I *am* a reasonable man and I understand the need for careful and discreet negotiations. But if you take that donkey out of this yard, I'll cut yer legs off!

P: *(To BARTHOLOMEW)* He *will* too, Bartholomew. Remember my friend's donkey?

B: *(To DAVE)* Of course, Dave, you do *realize* that there'll be thousands of people watching the donkey parade into Jerusalem. Think of the publicity – a thousand people watching *your* donkey with a banner saying 'This donkey was supplied by Dave's Donkeys'...

P: And still has all four legs.

B and D: Shut *up*!

D: It's a nice idea, but no. If you want the donkey, you'll have to pay for it. Now I can do you a very nice deal on this beaut – low mileage, only one careful owner...

P: And several careless ones by the look of it! Come on, Bartholomew, he's not going to give it to us. *(They start to leave.)* I told you, you should have said that *the Master* wanted it, just like Jesus told you to.

D: Jesus? Really? You should have said! Of course you can have it. Here, take it with you now. *(DAVE hands them the reins. PHILIP and BARTHOLOMEW start to leave. DAVE calls after them.)* Err... better still, take *this* one. *(DAVE points to one that's offstage.)* The one you've got there has a dodgy leg! *(PHILIP and BARTHOLOMEW let go of the reins of the first donkey and go off to collect the other one.)* And don't worry about rushing back – Jesus can borrow it for as long as he wants!

© CPAS 1996

God of the Details

DIRECTOR'S TIPS

TRAILER

Why leave Jesus out of the picture, when he's the one who knows everything and knows best?

Make Dave's Donkeys like a typical second-hand car dealer's place, with hand-painted signs and bunting.

Practise the timings of Philip's comments about donkeys having four legs and Bartholomew and Dave's replies. The sharper these are the funnier they will be.

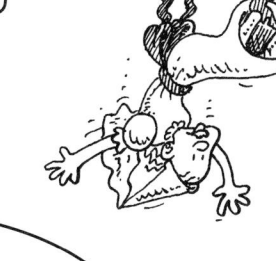

To make the 'donkey' look alive, Philip and Bartholomew need to make it move before they do. Rehearse moving the 'donkey' and then reacting to it, not the other way round.

WORKSHOP

Before the session, make several copies of **Matthew 21:4** on A4-sized paper. Cut these up into jigsaws. Put each jigsaw in a separate envelope, leaving out one of its pieces. Divide the group into pairs and give each pair an envelope. Tell them it's a race to complete the jigsaw. When they start to protest that there's a piece missing, tell them not to be so fussy but just to get on with it. Keep on insisting that they're worrying too much. Eventually give in, handing them the missing piece. Award prizes to the pair that finishes first.

Jigsaws are a complete waste of space without all the pieces. We have to pay attention to detail if we're going to complete the jigsaw. Bartholomew didn't worry about the details when he went to get the donkey from Dodgy Dave. He left out what Jesus had said, and getting the donkey nearly all went horribly wrong.

Look at **Matthew 21:1-9**, especially verses 4 and 5. God knew the details hundreds of years earlier, and the details were important.

Fortunately God – Jesus – still pays attention to detail, including the details of our lives. When something's bothering us (and even when *nothing* is!), it makes sense to ask the One who knows everything and who knows best about the details. Get everyone to write down one area of concern for them – at school, at home or out with their friends – and to pray in small groups being as specific as people are happy to be. Help everyone to be sure that Jesus cares about the details.

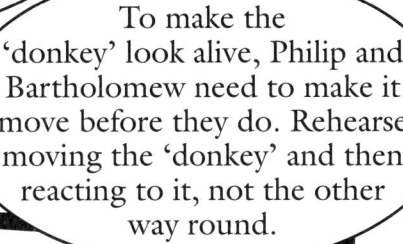

Veronica's Virulent Virus

VERONICA A teenager who's very ill
MAYOR who isn't ill at all
DOCTOR A doctor

(There are three chairs in a row in a doctor's waiting room. VERONICA is sitting on an end one. In the corner is a wastepaper bin. The MAYOR enters carrying a briefcase and wearing a hat. He takes his hat off.)

MAYOR: You don't mind if I sit here, do you?

VERONICA: No, not at all. *(Pause)* Aren't you the Mayor?

M: *(Sitting and putting his hat down on the chair beside him)* That's right. And you are?

V: Veronica.

M: Well, it's a pleasure for you to meet me, Veronica.
(They both wait looking bored.)

V: I don't suppose I could borrow your briefcase, could I?

M: Certainly. *(He hands VERONICA his briefcase which she puts on her lap. She opens it and is violently and loudly sick into it. She calmly closes it and passes it back to the MAYOR.)*

V: Thank you. *(The MAYOR takes his briefcase and is speechless.)*

DOCTOR: Next patient, please!

M: Ah, that'll be me. *(To VERONICA)* See you soon. *(He walks over to the doctor's desk.)* Good morning.

D: Good morning. Now then, what seems to be the problem?

M: Nothing.

D: Nothing?

M: No, I'm as fit as a fiddle. Never felt better!

D: Then why are you here?

M: Because I'm the Mayor and I knew you'd want to meet me.
(VERONICA has heard this and has crossed behind the MAYOR.)

V: Excuse me, but I just heard you say you aren't ill, so I wonder if I could... *(She suddenly dashes back to the wastepaper bin and throws up into it. Afterwards she looks relieved to have reached the bin in time.)*

M: Strange girl, bursting in here like that! No manners these youngsters. Now then, what were we saying? Ah yes, you'd like to meet me, on account of me being so important.

D: But I never asked to see you. *(VERONICA crosses behind the MAYOR again.)*

V: Excuse me, could I...? *(She dashes back to the bin and throws up again. She collapses into her chair.)*

M: Doctor, you really must do something to stop other people interrupting us.

D: But there's nothing wrong with *you*, and *she's* ill.

M: Well, she should get herself sorted out. Now then... *(VERONICA crosses over again.)*

V: Please can someone...? *(She dashes back to the bin, then realizes it's full. She clasps her hand over her mouth and looks around in panic. She goes for the MAYOR's briefcase, then remembers that it too is full. She looks around even more panic-stricken. She see the MAYOR's hat, grabs it and throws up into it, making sure the MAYOR can't see. She collapses into her chair again.)*

D: Look, you'll just have to look after yourself. That girl needs me. *(He rushes over to VERONICA and looks after her.)*

M: *(To the audience)* Well, how rude! You wonder what doctors are for some days, don't you?
(They all freeze.)

© CPAS 1996

Being Saved

DIRECTOR'S TIPS

> For some reason, young people think the sight and sound of someone throwing up is incredibly funny. So exploit this to the maximum throughout the sketch.

> The performer playing the part of Veronica should practise making the loud vomiting noises without straining her throat!

> When being sick, Veronica should make it more over-the-top each time, to increase the humour.

TRAILER

The doctor knew who *really* needed his help. So does Jesus. Will *you* accept his offer of help?

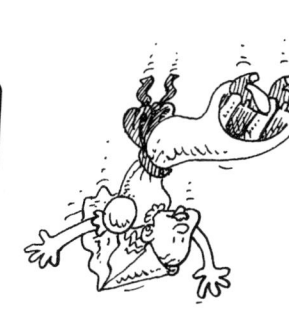

WORKSHOP

Point out how ridiculous it was for the Mayor to go to the doctor's for no reason. Not only was it stupid but it also wasted the doctor's time. The doctor should have been looking after Veronica who was ill.

Cut out from newspapers six pictures of different people. Try to get some contrasts – people celebrating, crying, old, young etc. Stick them round the walls of the room where you meet. Get the group to go round, look at the photos and decide which people in the pictures they would or wouldn't like to come to church. Discuss their answers together. Why did they choose some people and not others?

Read **Mark 2:13-17**. The Pharisees criticized Jesus for eating with tax collectors and sinners. They had a very clear idea about the kind of people he should be mixing with. But Jesus said the tax collectors and sinners were *exactly* the kind of people he should be mixing with because they needed his help, just as sick people need a doctor's help. Jesus hadn't come for people who thought they were righteous and perfect, but for those who knew they did things wrong and needed his forgiveness.

It's Happened!

JOHN, **PETER** and **HELEN** Three friends

(There's a chair on stage. JOHN and HELEN stand chatting amiably. From off stage we hear the sound of running feet followed by PETER shouting.)

PETER: JohnJohnJohnJohnJohnJohnJohnJohnJohnJohnJohnJohnJohnJohnJohnJohn JohnJohnJohnJohnJohnJohnJohnJohn! *(PETER eventually runs on stage still shouting. JOHN and HELEN ignore PETER until it's too late. At the last moment JOHN turns to see PETER who collides with him, knocking him to the ground. PETER gets up very excitedly.)* It's happened! It's happened! It's happened!

JOHN: I think his brain cell has finally arrived.

HELEN: Peter, what *are* you going on about?

P: It's finally happened after all these years – the waiting's over!

H: Well, that's lovely, but *what* has happened?

P: I can't believe it's true! It's so amazing!

J: Perhaps his voice has broken.

H: Why don't you just calm down and tell us *what* has happened?

P: Calm down? Calm down? On a day like this? Are you joking? This is the best day of my entire life!

J: It could be the *last* if you go on like this much longer.

(PETER starts waltzing round the stage singing Oh, What a Beautiful Morning! *to himself.)*

H: Oh, don't be so mean, John! He's just excited, that's all.

J: Yes, but what *about*?

H: Well, it must be pretty good news – just *look* at him!

J: Peter, Peter, Peter! *(PETER ignores all this.)* Hello? Earth calling Peter, Earth calling Peter, are you receiving me? Over! *(PETER scoops JOHN up into his dance and waltzes him off round the stage. HELEN collapses in laughter.)* Will you get *off* me? Let me go! Helen, *do* something!

H: *(Enjoying the spectacle)* Oh, but you make such a lovely pair!

J: Don't just stand there – call a doctor! Better still, a vet! *(PETER suddenly stops dancing and collapses into a chair.)*

P: Oh, what a lovely day! *(JOHN loses his temper, grabs PETER by the collar and pulls him up.)*

J: What are you so excited about?

P: Who? Me?

J: Yes, *you*! *(JOHN lets PETER go.)*

P: Oh, didn't I *tell* you? My hamster won first prize in the international championships!

H and J: *(Looking at each other disappointedly, pausing, then...)* Oh!

(They all freeze. PETER is stunned that JOHN and HELEN aren't thrilled.)

© CPAS 1996

Spreading the Good News

DIRECTOR'S TIPS

> Spend time rehearsing the visual humour, e.g. the knocking over and dancing. It will help make it all as funny as possible.

> Practise very carefully the disappointment and 'freeze' at the end.

> The performers need to be fit so that they're not gasping after their running and dancing. No one will hear them if they're trying to get their breath back.

TRAILER

Peter told everyone about his hamster because he was so excited about it. How excited are *you* about being a Christian?

WORKSHOP

Split the group into teams. Give each team a copy of the same newspaper. Ask them to find a particular headline and race to you to tell you the page number in the paper. Repeat this with a number of headlines.

Look at **Luke 2:8-20**, particularly verses 17 and 18. The shepherds wasted no time in telling other people about Jesus – it was the first thing they did. Make the connection between this, the teams racing to tell you their headlines, and Peter rushing to tell John and Helen his news in the sketch. All these people were excited about the news they'd received. Our task is the same as the shepherds' – to tell people as much as we know of the Good News of Jesus.

John and Helen weren't very excited by Peter's news. We don't know what everyone made of the news the shepherds brought, but the shepherds told people anyway. Our job is to *tell* people – God will deal with the results.

One Man and his Voice

COMMENTATOR
GRAEME The good shepherd
JEFF The bad shepherd

(The COMMENTATOR holds a microphone. JEFF and GRAEME stand close by waiting to be interviewed.)

COMMENTATOR: Well, here we are at the end of the Welsh Open Sheepdog Trials. It has been, I believe, the most dramatic and indeed unusual final since 1932 when a wolf, dressed as a sheep, got in and ate seven of the competitors. Anyway, just to recap on the scores here this afternoon... the champion Graeme gained the maximum one hundred points whilst his opponent Jeff scored a total of three. So first of all, Jeff, what went wrong for you today?

JEFF: The sheep. Stupid things just sort of ran about all over the place. They didn't really seem to know where they were going.

C: Which surely is the *point* of a sheepdog trial. So were these sheep different from those you're used to dealing with?

J: I don't know – I never even got to *eat* them. Usually I have sheep on a plate with some new potatoes and mint sauce... none of this stupid running about chasing them up and down hills.

C: Errr, yes... so... ummm... whilst you were trying to *eat* the sheep, what was your dog doing? She didn't seem very interested in what was going on. In fact, to put it politely, she was absolutely useless!

J: How *dare* you call Trixibelle useless! *She* just doesn't care for sheep either.

C: Errr... Right! Fine! *(JEFF exits.)* Now let's turn to Graeme, the victor, who scored the maximum one hundred points. A great afternoon for you, Graeme.

G: Yes, thanks mainly to the sheep. They were absolutely brilliant!

C: Which brings us on to your technique, which is rather unusual. Although this is a *sheepdog* trial, you don't actually use a dog, do you?

G: No, the sheep are so special and important I prefer to call them by name.

C: Now don't try to pull the wool over my eyes! You can't *really* call each one by name.

G: Certainly you can, if you treat them properly rather than chasing them around with dogs. Then they respond to your love and care for them.

C: I see... errr... Now at one point it looked as if you were going to lose one of your sheep. Would you like to talk us through what happened?

G: Yes. It was Joanna, the one with the longer fleece. She wanted to get into the next field – she thought there'd be better grazing there. Well, I knew she'd have to cross a deep river to get there, and she can't swim well. I didn't want her to hurt herself, so I rounded up the rest of the flock and went to bring her back.

C: And where *was* she when you found her?

G: Stranded on a rock in the middle of the river. So I swam out to her and brought her back to the rest of the flock.

C: *(To the audience)* For those of you who weren't with us earlier, I have to tell you that Graeme actually gave Joanna... errr... the sheep a piggyback up the hill.

G: A sheepyback! You give pigs piggybacks and sheep sheepybacks.

C: Of course. Silly me! So Graeme gave Joanna a... *sheepy*back up the hill and then walked round the course with the sheep. *(Pause)* Quite remarkable. *(Pause, then to GRAEME)* So do you have any tips for people at home who may be thinking of becoming shepherds? I mean, what makes a *good* shepherd?

G: The good shepherd knows his sheep by name. They recognize his voice and follow him. In the end, he's willing to lay down his life for his sheep.

C: Thank you, and now back to the studio.

(GRAEME and the COMMENTATOR freeze.)

© CPAS 1996

The Good Shepherd

DIRECTOR'S TIPS

Use costumes and props to give the sketch visual impact. The Commentator needs a microphone. Graeme could have a crook and Jeff a frying pan.

Jeff should be very critical of anything to do with sheep.

Make sure Graeme is sincere but not weird.

TRAILER

Jesus said, 'I am the good shepherd.' Would *you* recognize his voice?

WORKSHOP

Play 'Sheep and Shepherds'. Two teams line up in the middle of the playing area facing each other, with about two metres between the lines. Name one team 'sheep' and one 'shepherds'. Call out either 'sheep' or 'shepherds'. If you call out 'sheep', they have to chase the 'shepherds' to the side of the playing area. Any 'shepherds' they catch become 'sheep' and join that team. If you call 'shepherds', they have to try to catch 'sheep'. Play several rounds, calling the names out randomly. Later add some trick names like 'chef' or 'shears'. Anyone who moves when you say this has to swap sides.

Ask the group to say what they think was the most important thing about the game. It was crucial to listen carefully and to be ready to chase or run on the right command. If they didn't listen properly, they were likely to run the wrong way.

Look at **John 10:1-11**. Verses 1 to 4 explain that sheep follow the shepherd because they know his voice. Jesus said that he is the good shepherd. Think back to the sketch and the Bible verses, and get the group to identify characteristics of both the sheep and the good shepherd from it.

Jesus calls us by name. We need to recognize his voice and follow him.

United

'ARRY and **DAVE** City supporters
SID and **JOHN** Rangers supporters
As many other supporters for each team as you like!
NEWSPAPER SELLER

(Both groups of supporters enter from opposite sides chanting, singing and generally being rowdy.)

'ARRY: 'Ere, Dave! It's them bonehead Rangers supporters! *(To the opposing supporters)* Oi, Sid! What's a load of pollution like you lot doing around here?

SID: Looking for trouble, but we're not gonna waste our time hassling City wimps like you!

'A: Wimps? *Wimps?* No one calls us wimps and lives!

(Both sides square up to each other without actually making physical contact. Suddenly a NEWSPAPER SELLER runs on shouting the latest news. All the supporters freeze and listen.)

SELLER: Extra, extra! Read all about it! Rangers and City to merge! One new club called United to be formed! Extra, extra!

(The NEWSPAPER SELLER exits. The supporters pause, stunned by the news, then slowly and silently return to their respective sides.)

SID: Did I just hear what I thought I heard, John?

J: Yeah, you did.

SID: I thought so.

'A: Errrr... Things are looking grave, Dave.

D: Yeah, dead serious, 'Arry. *(He laughs at this own joke.)*

SID: What we gonna do about it then, eh?

'A: Stop hating each other?

SID: What? No more harassment?

'A: Could be.

(SID thinks about it. He's obviously very confused.)

SID: OK then – let's give it a go.

(The two groups of supporters cautiously sit down near each other.)

J: Our goalie did a brilliant save this afternoon.

D: Call that brilliant?

'A: Call that a goalie? I've seen more talent in a frog!

J: Yeah. Well, at least our team don't *look* like frogs!

D: You cheeky toad! You'll pay for that!

(Both groups of supporters square up to each other again. 'ARRY and SID come between them.)

SID: Hang on, hang on. We can't spend every Saturday afternoon causing each other grief like this.

J: Why not? We do now!

SID: 'Cos we're supposed to be on the same side, that's why.

'A: Well, we'll just have to not talk to each other, then there won't be any trouble.

(There are general murmurs of agreement. The supporters all mill around in silence trying to ignore each other. Eventually 'ARRY and JOHN come face to face with each other and gradually become more and more aggressive as they try to get past.)

'A: No, no. It's no good. Whatever we do, we just end up causing each other grief.

D: 'Ow about if we all try supporting the new team?

REST: *(Chanting)* Yer what? Yer what? Yer what? Yer what? Yer what?

D: Instead of trying not to hassle each other, let's all concentrate on supporting the new team. *(He starts chanting very cautiously.)* United, United... *(Gradually everyone else joins in until they're all chanting loudly. They exit still chanting and very obviously all friends.)*

© CPAS 1996

The Peace of God

DIRECTOR'S TIPS

If your group members are involved in acting, make sure the rowdiness doesn't get out of control as you rehearse!

The two groups of supporters should dress in distinctive colours.

The chants and shouts must die down quickly enough for the individual characters to be heard.

TRAILER

Can't believe it? God can even help enemies become friends.

WORKSHOP

Give every group member and leader two pieces of different coloured paper. Make everyone work on their own. Encourage honesty. Tell them not to write their names on the papers.

On one piece of paper they must write down something they like about the group or about a person in the group. On the other they must write something they dislike. Don't let them show each other what they have written – this will detract from the exercise.

Collect in the pieces of paper. Put them in two distinct piles – 'likes' and 'dislikes'. Write up all the 'likes' as quickly and as seriously as you can. When you have finished, reflect on them saying what a lot you have to thank God for.

Tear the other pile up. Although some of the things in this pile may be important, we should always concentrate on the things that draw us together, especially on Jesus. When we focus on the 'dislikes', we're working against the Holy Spirit who wants to bring peace.

Keep the 'dislike' sheets in your pocket after you have torn them up, to prevent your group members rummaging through the bin afterwards! To be sure of treating your group members with integrity, destroy the sheets without reading them yourself first.

Look at **Galatians 3:26-29** and **5:22-23** together. Peace between people is just one aspect of the amazing peace that God can bring into our lives.

The Court Case

JUDGE Obviously an idiot
POLICE SERGEANT Quietly efficient and monotonous
DEFENDANT Fairly innocent-looking

(The scene is a courtroom. The JUDGE is sitting in his judge's chair.)

JUDGE: *(Shouting)* Right, bring in the next case! *(The POLICE SERGEANT enters carrying a large suitcase and places it in front of the JUDGE.)* OK, leave this to me, sarge. I think I can handle this! Get it? *Handle* it.

SERGEANT: Yes, m'lud. Very amusing, m'lud.

J: Now then, what's the charge? *(Looking at papers)* Ah, impersonating foreign rucksacks without due care and attention. Well, it won't take us long to sort this one out. In fact it will be a *brief* case!

S: Very good, m'lud. *Brief* case. Ha, ha, ha!

J: And where did this terrible crime take place?

S: At Buckingham Palace, m'lud.

J: *(To the suitcase)* Ah, you want to be a *court* case, do you?

S: It is *now*, sir.

J: Pardon?

S: I caught it. It's a *caught* case. Get it?

J: Don't be so stupid, sergeant! *(To the suitcase)* Right, I sentence you to three weeks in Left Luggage at Waterloo Station, and I hope that'll be a lesson to you. Well, sergeant, that's another one *bagged*.

S: Yes, m'lud. Bagged. Very good.

J: *(Shouting)* Next! *(The DEFENDANT enters and stands on a chair.)* What the dickens are you doing up there? Come down at once.

DEFENDANT: But I thought this was a *high* court.

J: Right, that's a £32 fine for making jokes about court cases.

D: *(Getting off the chair)* But, but, but, but, but, but, but, but, but, but...

J: And that will be another £14.27 for repeating yourself over and over and over and over and over and over and over again.

D: *(Shouting)* You're not allowed to do that!

J: *(Shouting)* I am and I will. *(He becomes calm again.)* And what's more, that's another £38.41 you owe for shouting in court.

D: *(Scratching his head in disbelief)* But I haven't done anything wrong!

J: Haven't done anything wrong? Did you hear that, sergeant?

S: Yes, m'lud.

J: Ridiculous, isn't it?

S: *(Obviously agrees)* Errmmm... apparently so, m'lud.

D: *(Scratching his head in disbelief)* But it's *true*!

J: You've broken just about every rule in the book! *(The JUDGE scratches his armpit absent-mindedly.)* And it's my duty to inform you that scratching yourself in public is punishable by a fine of £142.93 payable at once.

D: But I haven't got any money.

J: No money? But you owe me... I mean the *court* £227.71. Crimes of scratching, shouting, repeating yourself and making jokes about the court have clearly been committed. Take the guilty party away, sergeant!

(The POLICE SERGEANT seizes the JUDGE and carries him off. The DEFENDANT walks free.)

© CPAS 1996

Hypocrisy

DIRECTOR'S TIPS

> It will be worth the effort to collect costumes and props to set the scene.

> Don't make the puns or the Judge's hypocrisy subtle. Emphasize the puns and allow time for the groans.

> The more straight-faced the Police Sergeant remains, the funnier the sketch will be.

TRAILER

It's easy to see faults in others. But what do we miss in ourselves?

WORKSHOP

Give everyone ten minutes to draw a self-portrait of themselves. Tell them they have to draw it from memory and not use any mirrors. When they have finished, bring a mirror in and let everyone have a look at themselves to see how well they did.

Explain that we're never very good at knowing what we look like, unless we spend hours studying ourselves in the mirror. We often draw ourselves how we would like to look – a more glamorous hairstyle, different shaped nose, fewer warts etc. The trouble with mirrors is that they show everything as it is. Jesus taught that it was really important to know what we're like on the *inside* too, and not assume we're perfect. The trouble with the Judge was he never checked his own behaviour.

Look at **Matthew 7:1-5**. Jesus didn't mess about with hypocrites – he had stern words for them, as he has for us too when we're hypocritical. Encourage everyone to spend time asking God to show them aspects of their life where they're being hypocritical and need to change.

Ananias, Where Are You?

ANANIAS

(ANANIAS enters and busies himself tidying up. He looks around as though he has heard someone calling his name. He tries to find out who it is by going to each side of the stage and calling 'Hello?' Finally he realizes it's God calling him.)

ANANIAS: Ah Lord, yes. Hello. Ananias your faithful servant here. *(He listens.)* Yes, sorry I didn't recognize your voice – I thought it was the neighbours complaining about the goat again. *(He listens again.)* Yes, Lord, I'm ready and listening.

Just one thing, Lord, if I could just check... Is this a genuine vision, or am I cracking up? *(He listens.)* It's a genuine one. OK, I'm ready. *(He listens with head bowed, then begins to look confused.)* Let me see if I've got this right. You want me to visit Saul of Tarsus and lay hands on him? I was right – I *am* cracking up. I'm off! *(He goes to leave. As he does so, he stops dead in his tracks as if God has commanded him to stop. He listens.)*

You *really* want me to go? *(He listens.)* Now hang on, are we talking about the same bloke here? Famous Jewish chap who stitches tents and *un*stitches Christians? *(He listens.)* We *are*? But this is the guy who thinks Christians make pretty tree decorations, if you know what I mean. *(He puts his arms out as if being crucified.)* He's the kind of bloke who goes to a party, has loads to drink and gets other people stoned. *(He listens, then starts to get worried and quite frantic.)*

Well, it's alright for *you*, but have you ever tried talking to him? *(He listens and suddenly looks embarrassed.)* Oh, you *have*? *(He gets worked up again.)* Yes, well, apart from that, the only thing a Christian ever manages to say to Saul is 'Please don't kill m...'. I mean, he's just not very good at making friends. Corpses, yes, but friends? No way! *(He listens carefully.)* You *really* want me to go? *(He listens and has an idea.)*

Well, OK. But how do I find this guy, other than waiting for a message personally delivered by machete? *(He listens.)* He's in a house on Straight Street. Straight Street? *Straight* Street? In the Roman Empire? That's hardly specific, Lord – there are millions of them! That's all they ever build, straight streets! *(He listens and feels foolish.)* Oh, Judas' house next door to our Linda's just round the corner. Oh yes, I forgot about *that* Straight Street. *(He listens much more calmly.)*

You'll definitely be with me? OK, I'll go then. Just let me get my coat. *(He listens.)* Yes, I *will* remember that you're there. Right! I'll see you soon. *(He turns to go and speaks to himself.)* Far *too* soon by the sound of it! *(ANANIAS exits.)*

Obedience

DIRECTOR'S TIPS

Make the listening most effective by imagining what God is saying. Pause for a different length of time on each occasion that God 'speaks'.

The performer should make God appear to be right there by always looking and talking to the same point, just above the audience's heads.

Make sure Ananias reacts with his voice, body and face to God's commands.

Rehearse this sketch well even though there's only one performer in it. If he or she dries up, there's no one to help out!

TRAILER

Ananias went to see Saul even though he was scared. How do *you* feel when you know there's something God wants you to do for him?

WORKSHOP

Have a general knowledge quiz. For the scoring have lots of pieces of paper with scores on. Turn the score sheets over so that no one can see the scores on them. When a team answers a question they pick a piece of paper to see how many points they have scored. On some of the pieces of paper put a forfeit which has to be accomplished before the team gets the points. The more embarrassing the forfeit, the more points the team gets.

Ananias had to decide whether to obey God or not. Look at **Acts 9:1-19**. Ananias really was scared about going to see Saul (vs.13-14). If your group knows the story well, including what Saul went on to do, ask them to imagine what might have happened if Ananias had refused to go.

The quiz included a zany way of choosing whether to obey commands or ignore them.

Being a Christian means more than just saying we love God – it also involves obeying his commands. Many of them are really difficult to obey, but they are *commands*, not just *suggestions*. We must aim to obey God as Ananias did, even when he asks us to do something we're afraid of.

Jesus had some pretty good things to say about people who obeyed God's commands (**Matthew 12:46-50**).

Conversation Pieces

(These short sketches may be performed all in one go, or at different points throughout a programme. In all the sketches JULIA, who's a Christian, is talking to IAN, who isn't.)

Part One

JULIA:	Ah, Ian. There you are. I was just wondering if I might share something with you.
IAN:	Ooo, thanks, Julia – I'm *starving*.
J:	Ha,ha! No, that's not what I meant. I want to share something about the gospel.
I:	You what?
J:	What you need to know, Ian, is where you're going.
I:	Well, I'm off down the shops actually.
J:	No. Where are you going *when you die*? Is Jesus living inside you?
I:	Well, I haven't noticed anyone setting up home in me tum, no!
J:	*(Getting annoyed)* Look, are you saved or aren't you?
I:	I don't know.
J:	Well, I suggest you come to church next week or God's gonna zap ya!

Part Two

(JULIA tries to 'relate' to IAN. She should try to copy any distinct postures, habits or actions of IAN's.)

J:	Ah, Ian, how's it going?
I:	Fine, thanks, Julia.
J:	That's brill! Just off to town then?
I:	Yep.
J:	Going to stock up on life's little luxuries, eh?
I:	Well, you *could* say that. I don't suppose you Christians have much money to spend, do you? Don't you have to give it all away?
J:	Oh no, not really. We put a bit in the old collection plate, but not if we don't want to. I *love* spending money actually.
I:	But you're not allowed to spend it on anything... fun, are you?
J:	Of course we are. Come to the group and you'll soon see we're just normal people.
I:	Well, I don't see much point if Christians are just the same as the rest of us.

Part Three

I:	Hi, Julia! Just been to church then?
J:	Errr... well... ummm... yeah, I suppose so.
I:	Good was it?
J:	It was OK.
I:	*(Interested)* What do you Christians get up to at church?
J:	What do we do? Well, we sort of sing and things.
I:	So what makes you want to go, then?
J:	Well, it's sort of good fun, and we learn some interesting things.
I:	*(Very interested)* Oh yeah? Such as...?
J:	Ummm, you know... we all... ummm... learn about Godandthingslikethat.
I:	*(Fed up with JULIA's lack of enthusiasm)* Well, it sounds dreadful! Next time I can't think of anything to do, I won't bother going to church either. *(He stomps off.)*

© CPAS 1996

Witnessing

DIRECTOR'S TIPS

Try not to make Julia appear too incompetent. She's doing better than many Christians.

Make the last line very clear each time. Performers shouldn't start walking off until they have finished saying it.

Add any relevant jokes or clichés that will appeal to your group, but don't send up anyone who might be offended.

TRAILER

If your friends asked why you went to church, what would you say?

WORKSHOP

Recap on the sketches pointing out where Julia got it right or wrong.

Part One: She got it right where she had the courage to talk about her faith, but wrong when she used complicated words and phrases, and lacked patience.

Part Two: She got it right when she tried to relate to Ian and understand him, but wrong when she made it sound as if being a Christian made no difference at all.

Part Three: She got it right when she actually told Ian about church, and only just got it wrong by understating what church was all about.

Have a look at **Acts 17:16-34**. Paul walked round the city and saw that people were religious but didn't know God. So he started to tell them. He was patient and explained things to them (link to *Part One*). He related to their way of life (link to *Part Two*). He wasn't embarrassed about being a Christian (link to *Part Three*).

Split the group into pairs and get them to work out a dialogue between Paul and the people of Athens. Advise them to keep their dialogues as short as the scenes between Julia and Ian.

The Soap Superstar

GLORIA GLORIOUS A soap superstar
KEVIN KETTLE An interviewer
IVANOSOCH A great drama teacher

	(KEVIN KETTLE sits on the set of a chat show. There are two vacant chairs.)
KEVIN:	Good evening, ladies and gentlemen, and welcome to *The World of Kevin Kettle*. Joining us later will be the queen of the soaps, the one and only Gloria Glorious. But first I'd like you to meet a man whose influence has affected us all, even though you may never have heard of him. He is, in fact, Gloria's drama tutor. Ladies and gentlemen, please welcome Mr Ivanosoch. *(IVANOSOCH enters.)* Good evening.
IVANOSOCH:	*(Taking one of the vacant seats)* Good evening.
K:	You're Gloria's drama teacher. How long have you had this *glorious* job? *(KEVIN laughs at the pun.)*
I:	Thirty-four years, since she started learning to act.
K:	Is she a good pupil?
I:	Not bad, not bad. She has learnt a lot, but still needs constant help and guidance for the roles she plays.
K:	Does she indeed? Because although you're her teacher, she rarely mentions you in public – which I think is a bit rotten. So let's ask the lady herself about it. *(To the audience)* Will you all please welcome Gloria Glorious? *(GLORIA enters in a very flamboyant fashion. She walks towards KEVIN, smiling at the audience, trips over and falls. KEVIN stands looking helpless. IVANOSOCH helps her up and into her chair.)*
GLORIA:	Good evening, Kevin darling.
K:	Good evening, Gloria. Now I was just talking to Ivanosoch your teacher. I was saying how little we hear of him. Why *is* that?
G:	Well, you know, lovey, some of us have talent, and others have funny Russian names. I'm afraid Ivan O'Socks got the name.
K:	But he's a great teacher. He has coached you through your whole career. You wouldn't be *anywhere* without him.
G:	Nonsense, darling. Ivan O'Socks is a lovely man, but has very little talent. I got where I am today by grit and determination, by the love of my fans, by my talent and desire for one thing – to make everyone smile. Now will you please stop going on about *him*! It's *me* you're supposed to be interviewing. Your viewers don't want to hear about *him*. It's *me* they love, *me*.
K:	OK. I gather you're about to star in a new stage production. Tell us all about that.
G:	Darling, I'm so glad you asked. It's that lovely little play *Romeo and Juliet* by...
I:	*(Aside to GLORIA)* William Shakespeare.
G:	William Shakespeare. I play Juliet who's madly in love with Romeo. There's this romantic balcony scene where Juliet is waiting for Romeo and she calls out to him. *(She gets up and overacts madly.)* Romeo, Romeo... *(She has forgotten her lines.)*
I:	*(Aside to GLORIA)* Wherefore art thou...?
G:	Wherefore art thou, Romeo? *(Sitting again)* Oh, Kevin, you *will* be at our opening night tomorrow, won't you? I've heard that Shakespeare himself hopes to come.
K:	Well, that should certainly be worth seeing. And Ivanosoch will be there?
G:	Don't be daft. Why should *he* be there?
K:	He directs the play.
G:	*(Innocently)* Really?
K:	Well, on that note I shall say thank you to Ivanosoch and Gloria Glorious for being with us this evening. I hope it all goes well tomorrow night. Gloria, I've just remembered that I'm washing my hair, so I won't be there. Sorry. This is me Kevin Kettle saying thank you and good night. Good night!

© CPAS 1996

Help from the Holy Spirit

DIRECTOR'S TIPS

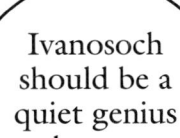

Ivanosoch should be a quiet genius who cares about Gloria.

Make Gloria as over-the-top as possible. She'll need confidence to ham up the acting, but the bigger and more dramatic she is, the better.

Kevin pronounces the name Ivanosoch perfectly, whereas Gloria mispronounces it, as 'Ivan O'Socks'. (By the way, it's pronounced Ivanosoch!)

Make sure everyone can see the performers' faces when they sit talking to each other.

TRAILER

We might think we're gifted, but where do our gifts come from?

WORKSHOP

Bring to the group a lot of different tools and DIY equipment, e.g. hammers, spanners, nails, pneumatic drill, but nothing too sharp and dangerous. Wrap them up as gifts. Give each group member one gift, or one between two if you have a large group, and get them to open it.

Then call out a list of tasks around the home that you need to do, e.g. put up a shelf. The young people individually or in their pairs have to decide whether their piece of equipment is needed for that job and, if so, bring it to you. Award points for correct items and deduct points for any that weren't needed for the job.

The gifts the Holy Spirit gives Christians are tools for building up the Church. Look at **1 Corinthians 12:1-11**.

Gloria thought she was hugely talented and gifted, but it was obviously Ivanosoch who had made her what she was. He had taught her everything and still helped her when she needed it. Christians all have different gifts to use, but there's no point in boasting about them because they are given by the Holy Spirit. It's him at work in Christians that enables them to do God's work. God should get all the glory.

In the game the tools were good for different purposes. Group members could only join in because they'd been given a tool. The Spirit gives different gifts to different people. Spend time recognizing and praying about the gifts that Christian group members and other church members have been given, and about how these gifts could be used in the Church. **Romans 12:3-8**, **Ephesians 4:1-13** and **1 Peter 4:7-11** will help with this.

The Perfect Sculpture

MONSIEUR LE PONCE A famous French artist
MABLE MOBBLE A fresh new artist
A STATUE

(The STATUE stands on a chair and is completely covered with a white sheet. MABLE is adjusting the sheet and making final preparations. MONSIEUR LE PONCE enters.)

MABLE: Ah, Monsieur Le Ponce, I'm so glad you could come to view my masterpiece.

LE PONCE: Ah, bonjour, ma petite souffle, Mable Mobble! Eet ees une grande delight to be 'ere, although I 'ave never 'eard of you before, Mable Mobble.

M: Well, this is my first ever work of art.

LP: Your first? But I was led to believe that I would see une statue très, très, très magnifique.

M: Oh, you will, you will. I may be new, but I have natural talent. My greatness comes from within, not from being taught.

LP: Then where ees ze masterpiece?

M: It's over here under this sheet, Monsieur. I'm very privileged that you've taken time off from your latest work to come and admire my brilliant... errr... latest creation. You won't be disappointed, I can assure you. After today, the word on the street will be that Monsieur Le Ponce has discovered Mable Mobble.

LP: Eet ees, Mable Mobble... 'ow you say?... une plaisure. 'Owever, I cannot stay for long as I 'ave to return to my studio to finish my work. I em doing une statue très importante for ze Président des United States.

M: The American President! Whew! Still, I can guarantee that this won't be a waste of your time, because this is one of the best statues ever. It's absolutely brilliant – it's so life-like, I don't know how I did it... errr... I mean, it's absolutely perfect. It'll blow your mind!

LP: *(Losing his temper)* Well, may we 'ave a look at ze sculpture, please, Mable Mobble?

M: What? Oh, of course, yes, yes! Let's look at the perfect sculpture. I tell you, you're going to be so impressed – it's absolutely stunning.

LP: Will you please get on with it?

M: OK, if you're ready, I shall reveal the masterpiece that's going to rock the art world. *(MABLE pulls the sheet off with a dramatic flourish.)*

LP: Ees this your idea of une joke, Mable Mobble? I thought you said eet was formidable!

M: What? You mean you don't think it's perfect, Monsieur Le Ponce?

LP: Perfect, Mable Mobble? I 'ave seen greater perfection dans une nursery!

M: *(Disappointed)* Oh! Well, what's wrong with it?

LP: Do you 'ave a few spare days whilst I tell toi, Mable Mobble? No, look – I will point out where you 'ave goan wrowng. *(LE PONCE begins to point out all the STATUE's faults by referring to the physical characteristics of the person playing the STATUE. For example, 'Nobody has arms that long!', 'What were you thinking of when you did the hair?', 'When are you going to finish the nose?', 'Why are the legs such an odd shape?')*

M: So, do I take it you're not interested in buying my work, Monsieur Le Ponce?

LP: You assume most correctly, Mable Mobble. This monstrosity ees not feet for sale. Ze best thing you can do ees throw eet dans le bin. Au revoir. *(He exits with a flourish.)*

M: And I thought it was absolutely perfect! *(She exits dejectedly.)*

© CPAS 1996

What Will We Be Like in Heaven?

DIRECTOR'S TIPS

- Use this sketch at the start of the session, so that the Statue can be in place and covered up before the group arrives.

- Exaggerate the French accent, but make sure everyone can still understand what Le Ponce says.

- When pointing out faults in the Statue, don't point out features that clearly *are* a bit embarrassing for the performer. This would be particularly hurtful.

- Make sure the performer playing the part of the Statue chooses a pose he or she can hold for a long time.

TRAILER

You might think you're pretty perfect, but who's judging?

WORKSHOP

Do the 'Binocular Relay Race'. Split the group into teams and give each team a pair of binoculars. Mark out a course using masking tape, or something else that won't damage the floor surface. Team members take it in turns to follow the course by only looking through the *wrong* end of the binoculars.

The trouble with looking through binoculars the wrong way is that everything appears to be far away and not very clear.

Focus on **1 Corinthians 13:8-13**. Explain to the group that these verses are about heaven, about the time when everything will be perfect. Get the group members to list the things that will vanish and the things that will remain in heaven. What does this tell us about what heaven will be like? Explain that there won't be any more 'tongues', 'knowledge' and 'inspired messages' because we'll know everything we need to know and will worship God face to face.

Heaven is going to be very different to earth, but we'll never *really* understand what it will be like until we get there. Mabble Mobble thought her sculpture was perfect, until it was checked by Monsieur le Ponce. We might think we're pretty perfect, or have seen, done or experienced amazing things, but this is nothing compared to heaven. While we're on earth we only catch glimpses of heaven, like something seen through binoculars the wrong way round, or in a dirty mirror. Explain to the group that, at the time the Bible was written, mirrors would probably have been made of polished bronze not glass, so the reflections would have been very poor.

Manic Mike's Paranoia Problem

BEN Very humble and controlled
MIKE Lacking in self-control

(There are two chairs on stage – a comfy one and a hard one. BEN enters eating some sweets. MIKE enters from the other side, sees BEN and holds out his hand as if expecting payment.)

MIKE:	*(Commanding)* My sweet!
BEN:	Ooooh, hello, deary!
M:	What?
B:	You called me 'my sweet', so I called you 'deary'.
M:	No – my *sweet*. I was asking for my sweet.
B:	Oh, right. Help yourself. *(MIKE snatches a sweet and eats it greedily. He's very satisfied with himself.)* Do you want another one?
M:	Eh?
B:	Would you like another sweet?
M:	Why, what's wrong with them?
B:	Nothing. I just thought you might like another one.
M:	Are you trying to make me sick?
B:	No, I just thought you…
M:	I know *your* game! You're trying to make me sick so you can tell the world how weak I am.
B:	No… really… I just thought you might like another sweet.
M:	Get away from me! You can't threaten me with a packet of sweeties! There's a law against *that* sort of thing, you know.
B:	Oh well, I'm sorry. Look, let's forget about the sweets, shall we?
M:	Forget? *Forget?* You stand there in broad daylight threatening me with a packet of sweets and you're asking me to *forget* it?
B:	Tell you what – let's just sit down and relax.
M:	Are you trying to tell me I'm not relaxed? I'm famous for my relaxing. People say, 'Look, there goes Mike – he looks relaxed!' I'M ALWAYS RELAXED!
B:	Well, *I'm* going to sit down anyway. *(BEN sits down on the hard chair.)* Why don't you have the comfy chair?
M:	Oh no, you're not going to trick me like that.
B:	Like *what?*
M:	I bet you've put a whoopee cushion under the seat.
B:	No, I haven't – try it!
M:	No way! I told you, I'm not going to fall for that one. I know what you're up to. First you try to attack me with a packet of sweeties and now the whoopee cushion. What have you got against me, eh?
B:	Nothing. I was just trying to…
M:	Why *me*, eh? What have I done to make you plot against me? Who knows what evil schemes you're hatching?
B:	All I said was, 'Why don't you have the comfy chair?'
M:	There you go again, trying to trap me. Well, I've had enough. I can't stand any more! I'm leaving you, do you hear?
B:	Pardon?
M:	I'M LEAVING! *(He storms off.)*
B:	I do hope he'll be alright. He does get worked up about things. *(He finishes eating the sweets, then exits.)*

© CPAS 1996

Self-Control

DIRECTOR'S TIPS

Mike needs to build up his fury until he's over-reacting to everything, but make sure he can still be heard even when he's worked up.

Build the fury towards the two points where the words are in capitals. These should be his biggest outbursts.

Ben should be relaxed but not unconcerned for Mike.

TRAILER

Some people say self-control is boring, but how much good does it do to lose it?

WORKSHOP

Split the group into pairs and get them to describe the temperament of Ben and Mike. Write up their answers so everyone can see. Discuss the differences. Emphasize that it was Ben's self-control that enabled him to remain calm whilst Mike went out of control.

Look at **Galatians 5:22-26**. Ask the group to answer these questions:

Who produces self-control in us (v.23)?

What must we let the Spirit do (v.25)?

What must we get rid of (v.24)?

Discuss what we can do about being more self-controlled. Encourage the group members to think what causes them to lose their self-control (people, situations etc.) and how they can best avoid or deal with these situations. Explain to the group that you yourself lose your self-control sometimes (if you do!) – it's something that happens to all of us, but the Holy Spirit can change us as we allow him to control our lives.

End with prayer.

You've Been Warned!

(These sketches may be performed all in one go, or at different points throughout your programme.)

Part One: The Fight

JOHN
DAVE

JOHN:	Oi, Dave!
DAVE:	Hello, John.
J:	Could you stand here like this for us? *(JOHN demonstrates standing with his legs apart and his arms flung wide.)*
D:	What, like *this*? *(He copies JOHN.)*
J:	Yeah, that'll do. Now don't move. *(JOHN starts to size DAVE up. He goes to punch DAVE in the stomach, but DAVE dodges and JOHN misses.)*
D:	Hang about! What's going on?
J:	Don't move! Get back where you were. *(DAVE gets back into position.)* I'm about to beat you up, so could you just stand still, please?
	(They freeze with JOHN about to hit DAVE.)

Part Two: The Flight

CHECK-IN CLERK
MR FIELDER An air passenger

	(MR FIELDER arrives at an airport check-in desk with his luggage.)
CLERK:	Good morning, sir. May I see your passport and tickets? *(MR FIELDER hands them over.)* Thank you. Luggage on the scales, please. *(MR FIELDER puts his luggage next to the desk.)* That's fifteen kilos – fine! Now, smoking or non-smoking?
MF:	Non-smoking, please.
C:	Window seat?
MF:	Yes, please.
C:	*(Handing MR FIELDER his tickets and passport)* There we are. Please proceed to Boarding Gate 7. I hope you have a pleasant flight.
MF:	*(Turning to go)* Thank you.
C:	Oh, and one last thing, Mr Fielder... This flight is due to be hijacked.

Part Three: Thief in the Night

SECRETARY
MRS JONES

	(The two performers mime speaking into a telephone.)
SECRETARY:	Good afternoon. Could I speak to Mrs Jones, please?
MRS JONES:	Hello. Speaking.
S:	Ah, Mrs Jones. I'm just phoning to let you know that one of our representatives will be calling at about ten past midnight tonight. So if you could leave your doors unlocked and the silver on the table, that would be a great help.
MJ:	I'm sorry? *Who* did you say would be calling?
S:	One of our representatives.
MJ:	And who *are* you exactly?
S:	Oh, didn't I say? I *am* sorry. I'm calling on behalf of Happy Home Burglaries Ltd. *(Both characters freeze.)*

© CPAS 1996

Jesus' Return

DIRECTOR'S TIPS

> These sketches are very short, so make sure you establish the characters quickly with props, costumes and clear delivery of the lines.

> The last line in each sketch is vital, so make sure it's slow, loud and clear.

> The performers should hold the 'frozen' poses for about five seconds, to give the sketches strong, clear endings.

TRAILER

No one knows when Jesus is coming back. It will be bad news for some people. Will you be ready for it by being on God's side now?

WORKSHOP

Get the group to stand absolutely still. Tell them they mustn't move until you clap your hands. When you do so, they have to run to the other end of the playing area. The first one there will get a sweet. If anyone wobbles or starts to move before you have actually clapped, they're out. Have a few goes at this, varying the length of time they have to wait before you clap your hands.

Point out that, in the game, it was no good running early or not concentrating on standing still. You had to be ready for the clap, whenever it came. In the three sketches, different people heard about bad things that were about to happen. Ask the group what they think the people should have done to get out of the situations. The people could have done something because they'd been warned, just as the group had been warned about the rules of the game.

Explore **1 Thessalonians 5:1-11**. Divide the group in half. With the Bible verses to guide them, ask one half to describe what Jesus' return will be like for people who *aren't* on God's side, and the other half what it will be like for people who *are* because they trust in Jesus. Compare the different answers.

Make the point that we haven't a clue *when* Jesus will return but we definitely know he will, so we need to be ready. Bring out the assurance of verses 9 and 10 and, using verses 8 and 11, encourage the group to think about how we can be ready.

To Work or Not to Work

MR GRIMES The Teacher
CHRIS, JO and **ANDY** His pupils

	(The pupils are sitting at their desks.)
GRIMES:	Good afternoon, class. Today we shall study French imperfect conjunctive pronouns.
JO:	*(Very fed up)* Oh, whoopee!
G:	Pardon?
J:	Errrr... I said, 'Mais oui', Mr Grimes.
G:	Hmmmmm? Now, I shall be setting you an exercise to do unsupervised – I have an urgent meeting with the head. *(All the pupils cheer.)* However, I expect you to concentrate on your work and, just in case anyone is thinking of sneaking off, I shall be back before the end of the lesson. So turn to page vingt, neuf, trois, sept, cinq of your books *Xavier Goes Snail Hunting* and answer questions 14 to 793. I shall want them all finished by the end of the lesson. *(He picks up his bag and leaves. There's silence for about fifteen seconds while the pupils work.)*
ANDY:	Jo, Jo, can you do *any* of this?
J:	No, I don't know anything about French, except *(said in a very bad French accent)* 'Bonjour, mon sewer'.
A:	I don't reckon old Grimes will be back this afternoon, so there's no point in doing this rotten old French rubbish.
J:	Yeah, I bet he's gone for a fag.
A:	Or off home. Yeah, he's skived off! Look, he's taken his bag.
J:	Narr, he's gone to chat up Miss Hipkiss. Did you see the way they sat next to each other in assembly?
A:	Yeah... Oi, Chris! What are you doing?
CHRIS:	Working.
J:	Oh, don't be so boring! Grimesy isn't coming back this afternoon.
C:	Don't be stupid! He *said* he'd be back.
J:	Who are you calling stupid?
C:	Look, just get on with the work. He'll be back soon. He always does what he says.
A:	Well, if you're so clever, what's the answer to number 16?
C:	Number 16? What happens to dead French hats? Oh, come on, that's easy! You *beret* them. I think it's Grimes's idea of a joke.
A:	Well, mercy buckets, I'm sure.
J:	*(Pause. JO suddenly recalls the previous conversation. To CHRIS)* So why *has* old Grimesy taken his bag then?
A:	Perhaps the head wants to give him le sac! *(ANDY and JO laugh stupidly.)*
J:	He's probably gone to take Miss Hipkiss a bunch of garlic.
A:	Or to show her his frog's legs!
J:	*He's* blinkin' got frog's legs. I bet he hops everywhere!
C:	He'll hop on you two if you don't get this finished.
A:	*(Losing his temper)* Will you shut up? The lesson's nearly over – he won't bother coming back now, so stop going on about it.
J:	Come on, Andy. If we go now, we'll get to the shops before the others.
A:	Yeah, OK. Coming, Chris? Narr, I s'pose you're going to stay and swot for Teacher. *(JO and ANDY go to leave. They bump into GRIMES coming back.)*
G:	And just where do you think *you're* going?
A:	Errrr... It was Chris. He said you wouldn't come back so we might as well go home.
J:	That's right – it was Chris's fault.
G:	Well, there's an easy way to check this out. I want you all to show me your books. *(They all show GRIMES their books.)* I think, Chris, that you can go early today. *(CHRIS leaves. GRIMES turns angrily towards JO and ANDY. All freeze.)*

© CPAS 1996

Preparing for Jesus' Return

DIRECTOR'S TIPS

Find places where Jo and Andy can stand up and sit down.

Make sure the desks are at a slight angle so that all the pupils can be seen and heard.

Chris needs to keep working hard throughout the sketch.

Build up Andy's anger throughout the sketch until he loses his temper with Chris at the end.

TRAILER

Jesus said he'd come back. Until he does, will *you* keep on working and living God's way?

WORKSHOP

Play 'Hidden Treasure'. The group sits in a circle and one member goes out of the room. Give a watch to someone in the rest of the group. He or she has one minute to hide it somewhere about their person. When the minute is up, call in the person from outside, who must now try to guess who has the watch. As a distraction, other members can act as if they have it. The guesser is only allowed three guesses. If he or she guesses correctly, the guesser has another go. If not, someone else goes out of the room.

Point out that people hid the watch and behaved in a particular way because they knew the person was going to come back in. In the sketch, Chris carried on working because he was sure Grimes would be back.

Look at **1 Thessalonians 1:2-3**. The Christians in Thessalonica had a firm hope in Jesus. Ask the group what the Thessalonians did as a result of this. They put their faith into practice and worked hard because of their love for Jesus.

Before reading out the whole of **1 Thessalonians 4**, ask the group to imagine they're the Thessalonian Christians. Warn them that they'll need to answer the following question at the end of their listening: Because Jesus is coming back, what *other* changes do you need to make in the way you live? Now read the verses dramatically and get the group to answer the question.

Jesus has said he will return, so we know he *will*. We need to get ready by putting our faith into practice.

Split into small groups and discuss times when it's hard to live God's way. Compile answers from the small groups. So, *at those times*, how can we can put our faith into practice so that we're ready for Jesus' return?

The Challenge

URGLE and **SQUORN** Two demons

        (URGLE and SQUORN are looking down on imaginary people and commenting on the scene.)

URGLE: Squorn, how horrible to see you!

SQUORN: Urgle, you mouldy old lump, it's revolting to see *you* again!

U: What vile things have you been up to then?

S: Oh, just the usual – annoying people, testing people and... errr... *(Smiles devilishly) tempting* people.

U: You've learnt to *do* that now, have you? I remember you being bottom of the class in tempting lessons when we were at Devil Hill School for Young Demons.

S: Yeah, well, I can tempt humans as well as the best demons now. I bet I'm even better than you, Urgle.

U: Oh yeah? Right, we'll try you out then. Best of three and you can go first.

S: You're on. Now then, who shall I pick on? *(He looks down at the imaginary humans.)* Ah, there's Ian now. *(Calling)* Ian, your mum has left her purse open and it's full of lovely money. *(To URGLE)* He's seen the purse, he's not sure what to do. *(Calling)* Don't forget, you're going out with your mates tonight and they'll all have money. Karen likes a bloke with a bit of cash to spare. *(To URGLE)* The defences are down – it's nearly all over. *(Calling)* Go on, Ian! Open the purse, take the money! Your mum won't notice. Don't just take the change, get in there among the notes. That's it – take the lot! *(Shouting)* You've done it! *(To URGLE)* You see? No problem! Your turn.

U: OK, let's find a suitable victim. Ah, there's Sharon about to meet up with her school mates. She's got some juicy gossip she promised she wouldn't spread! *(Calling)* Hey, Sharon, there are all your mates and they haven't heard about Jan and Simon. You'll be really popular if you're the first to tell them. Don't worry about Jan – she'll never find out. *(To SQUORN)* This shouldn't be too hard. She's not sure what to do. Everyone's asking if she knows anything. She's hesitating. *(Calling)* Go on, tell them! They'll find out soon enough anyway. Far better for *you* to explain everything. That's it – now you've started you might as well give them all the gory details. Tell them about Friday night – a bit of exaggeration never hurt anyone. *(Cheering)* Well done! You've made it. I won! Easy, easy, easy!

S: Hang on – it's only one all. Look, there's Jan. She's heard what Sharon said. First one to make them fight wins.

U: You're on! *(Calling)* Jan, there's that rat who said she was your friend. And now she's told everyone else about you and Simon.

S: *(Calling)* And you know what she's like – she's bound to have exaggerated things. Everyone will be laughing! That girl needs a good lesson. Kicking would be a start.

U: She's wavering – we could be onto a winner. Hang on – she's thinking about it.

S: Eeeeerrggh, how revolting! *(Calling)* Don't think – just hit her, Jan! She deserves it!

U: *(Calling desperately)* Yeah, punch her one now that her back's turned! Don't wait – go on! *(To SQUORN)* Here, Squorn, what's she doing?

S: We're in trouble now – she's praying!

U: *(Trying to call out but with no sound coming out)* Hey, Squorn, what's happened? My voice has stopped.

S: It won't work, will it? She's been praying for the strength to resist our tempting. Our voices won't get through to her now. Look, she's started talking to Sharon – she's even joking about what Sharon said. Makes you sick, doesn't it?

U: Oh, come on – let's go. There's no point hanging around now that they're all pally. And anyway, we *know* I'm the best.

S: What do you mean, *you're* the best?

        (They walk off arguing.)

Temptation

DIRECTOR'S TIPS

> Urgle and Squorn are two demons. The performers should use their imagination when choosing appropriate costumes, but pitchforks, horns and pointed tails may undermine the serious message of the whole sketch.

> When tempting the people, they should make it appear as if they can see the action happening below them. Both performers should look towards the same point, where the action is supposed to be taking place.

> Make the description of the action sound like the commentary for a football match.

TRAILER

Next time you're tempted to do something wrong, will you just give in or call for help?

WORKSHOP

Ask for four volunteers who would like to win a prize if they can keep totally quiet for two minutes. Sit them at the front so that everyone can see them. Assure them that the prize is really good – you'll tell them what it is at the end of the two minutes. Start the timer, then you and any other leaders you may have should try to persuade them to talk. Do this by offering them sweets or money if they'll just say 'Please', or by threatening to squirt them with a water pistol unless they say 'Stop!' Keep up the pressure for the full two minutes. Anyone who succeeds gets the star prize which must be, for example, at least £2 or a big box of chocolates.

After the activity, get the four volunteers to tell the rest of the group what it was like constantly being tempted to speak. Ask them why they did or didn't give in. Draw out how people give in to temptation because they can't take the pressure, they think there's a better offer, or they just stop concentrating and make a mistake.

Look at **James 1:12-15**. James explains that, in the end, it can actually be good for us to be tempted and to stand firm, but James knew it wasn't easy. Jan knew how to stand up to temptation – she prayed for strength. We need to do the same.

Spend time praying in groups for the strength to resist temptation.

The Pat Rowaneyes Show

PAT ROWANEYES A smug chatshow presenter
BILL LEAF Belle's husband, carrying an umbrella and dressed in wellingtons, cagoule and possibly swimming trunks
BELLE LEAF Bill's wife, carrying a handbag and wearing a very posh dress and nice jewellery
A GANG of waterpistol-bearing hoodlums

(It's yet another chat show, with two vacant chairs and one for PAT ROWANEYES, the host. PAT rushes on smiling inanely and waving to his adoring fan.)

PAT: Good evening, ladies and gentlemen, and welcome to *The Pat Rowaneyes Show*. That's me – Pat Rowaneyes. My first guests tonight claim to believe some quite outrageous things. So, without further ado, please give a big hand to Bill and Belle Leaf! *(BILL and BELLE enter and sit down.)* Welcome! Now before we mention your new book, let's talk about your rather interesting beliefs. Bill, let's start with you.

BILL: Well, Pat, my main belief is that we're going to get wet very soon. My other belief is that our new book will be a best seller.

P: So you seriously believe we're going to get wet very soon? *(He pauses and looks round in mock fear.)* Well, we seem to have survived so far! Let's hope it lasts for the rest of the show, eh? *(He laughs patronizingly.)* Now, Belle, turning to you for a moment, do you share your husband's beliefs?

BELLE: Oh yes, Pat. I believe all Bill says.

P: Hmmmm, I see. Yet you don't seem to have taken the same precautions as Bill?

BE: Well, you have to look your best on telly, don't you? Otherwise, what would the neighbours think? Besides, I've got an umbrella in my handbag here just in case.

P: Very wise, Belle. Aren't *you* worried about your appearance, Bill?

BI: Not really. You see, when we all get wet, I'll be ready and it won't spoil any of my clothes or anything. I've also brought along a waterproof copy of our latest book *Drips I Have Known*.

P: You really take this water thing seriously, don't you, Bill?

BI: Oh yes.

P: Well, so do *we*, don't we, ladies and gentlemen? I can see one lady in the audience has brought her snorkel with her. *(Calling out)* Very wise, love! You never know when you might need it. *(PAT laughs at his own joke. BILL puts up his umbrella.)* Oh, I see you've brought along a prop for tonight's show, Bill.

BI: Yes, well, I'm getting ready for the water, and I also wanted you to see the umbrella that features on the cover of our latest book.

P: Yes, well, first I must ask Belle if she really believes we're going to get wet.

BE: Oh yes. *Bill* says we are.

P: In that case shouldn't you be doing something about it? I mean, Bill might look a bit of an idiot, but people will find it hard to believe that *you're* quite as serious about your beliefs.

BE: Oooh, I don't know why. I mean, if Bill says we'll get wet, I believe it wholeheartedly.

P: Bill, we're nearly out of time. Still believing in the water?

BI: Yes, Pat.

P: *(Looking around again in mock worry)* Well, Bill, I'm afraid time has caught us up before the water did... *(As he says this, a GANG of waterpistol-bearing hoodlums rush on stage creating lots of noise and making PAT, BILL and BELLE as wet as your circumstances allow. PAT and BELLE try to defend themselves whilst BILL just sits there letting it happen. After the GANG has gone, BILL calmly puts down his umbrella. PAT and BELLE look very annoyed.)*

BI: *(To BELLE)* Come on then, love. It's time we were going.

P: You, you, you swine! Why didn't you tell me this was going to happen?

BI: I did, but you wouldn't believe me.

(BILL and BELLE exit. PAT sits looking very fed up.)

© CPAS 1996

Belief and Action

DIRECTOR'S TIPS

If you use this sketch in a group session, give the performers time to go and change before and after the sketch.

Don't use microphones – they don't like water.

Make sure you give time for shrieks or cheers to die down after the Gang squirts the water and before Pat and Bill say the last few lines.

Bill needs to look ridiculous, but be very sincere.

TRAILER

The way Bill behaved, showed us what he believed. What does the way you live say about what *you* believe?

WORKSHOP

Ask for one or two brave volunteers and blindfold them. Persuade them to stand on a chair in the middle of the room. Tell them that, on the command 'Go!', they should take one step forward, but promise that they won't fall or hurt themselves. Ask them if they believe you or not. As they're answering, quietly put another chair in front of them. Then give the command.

Whether or not the volunteers said they believed you, point out that they *must* have, otherwise they'd still be standing on the chair. Their belief meant that they *did* something.

Ask the group who they thought was the most sensible person in the sketch. If they say Bill, ask if they'd be prepared to go on TV dressed like that. Would they if they shared Bill's beliefs?

Look at **James 2:14-18**. James makes it clear that being a Christian is more than just saying we believe in Jesus. We have to *do* something about it and *live* as if we believe in him. We may look silly sometimes, but people will often judge what we believe by the way we behave.

Too Good To Be True

RAY GUNN A very charming, smooth-talking car salesman
MRS THRING A car lover
MECHANIC

(RAY GUNN is sitting at a desk on which there's a telephone and notepad. MRS THRING enters.)

MRS THRING: Ermmm... good morning. Is this the place that advertized the Porsche for sale in the local paper?

RAY GUNN: That's right. How may I help you?

T: Well, I rang yesterday and arranged to come and see the car today.

RG: What name is it, please? *(He starts to look through the notepad.)*

T: Thring. *(Pause – no response from RAY GUNN)* Thring, Thring!

RG: *(RAY GUNN thinks it's the phone and picks it up.)* Hello? Hello? Huh! They've hung up. Now then, what did you say your name was?

T: Thring, Thring – it's Mrs Thring!

RG: *(Going for the phone again)* Oh I see! *(He looks at the phone, then at MRS THRING and laughs.)* I'm terribly sorry – you must think I'm very rude. Please take a seat. *(MRS THRING sits down.)* Now you say you've come about the car?

T: Yes, that's right.

RG: Well, let me introduce myself. I'm Mr Raymond Gunn, but I prefer to be called Ray.

T: Ray Gunn?

RG: Yes indeed, and I'm the senior sales manager here. Now it was the red Porsche Turbo you were interested in, wasn't it?

T: Oooh, yes.

RG: Well, there *has* been a lot of interest in the car – hardly surprising really. It's not every day that a car in this condition comes on to the market at such a reasonable price. Only three years old and just one careful owner.

T: Has it done many miles?

RG: Hardly any at all – it's quite incredible really! And the bodywork's immaculate. It looks as though it's never been driven! I must say, you've been very sensible to come to the office. We've had so many people just phoning up but, with a car like this, it's so important to meet the customer. Do you have *another* car, Mrs Thring?

T: I've got a small car I use for work, but I really want this for the weekends.

RG: So very sensible, Mrs Thring. I wish there were more people like yourself who really respected cars. I can guarantee that you'll be amazed by this Porsche. As I say, it's in immaculate condition.

T: Yes, well, judging by the photo in the paper, it's perfect. *(She pauses, obviously thinking.)* I've made up my mind – I'll take it. It's too good an opportunity to miss. Here's my card. *(She hands RAY GUNN a credit card. He looks at it and writes down all the relevant information. MRS THRING then signs for the car.)*

RG: Thank you very much, Mrs Thring. It's been a pleasure doing business with you. Now, if you'd just like to wait here, I'll get someone to bring your car round. *(RAY GUNN exits. A few seconds later a MECHANIC enters carrying a toy Porsche which is hidden from view.)*

MECHANIC: Mrs Thring?

T: Yes?

M: Here's your Porsche. *(He puts the toy Porsche on the table and exits. MRS THRING looks at the car, horrified.)*

© CPAS 1996

Recognizing the Enemy

DIRECTOR'S TIPS

Ray Gunn should be really very nice – not smarmy, but pleasant and caring. Hopefully the audience too will be taken in by him.

Mrs Thring should like and trust Ray Gunn right up until the moment she sees the toy car.

Make sure all the audience can see the toy car.

TRAILER

Satan can disguise himself as an angel. Are you watching out for him?

WORKSHOP

Ask the group to draw the perfect spy, labelling all the necessary qualities needed, e.g. big shoes for hiding secrets in, x-ray eyes, big head for learning twenty-seven languages.

Display the pictures and decide which is the most important quality. Suggest that perhaps the most important quality for spies is to be able to convince people they don't exist. If no one thinks they exist, they won't try to stop them, and the spies can do whatever they like.

Mr Gunn convinced Mrs Thring that he was a genuine salesman. She had no idea he was really a con-man. If she'd known, she would have treated him very differently.

Look at **2 Corinthians 11:14**. Paul says that Satan can disguise himself as an angel of light. He can convince people that he's OK *really* – or even that he doesn't actually exist! Ask your group members if they think he has been successful in doing this. We need to recognize, as Jesus did, that Satan does exist and is dangerous, but we're not left alone to stand against him. **Ephesians 6:10-18** explains that God gives us all the protection and support we need. Our job is to stand firm and to pray.

Spend time praying that you and your group members will always be able to recognize Satan's lies and cons, and resist them knowing that Jesus has already won the victory over him.

Bible Index

Reference	Page	Title / Subtitle
Genesis 17:15-19; 21:1-7; 22:1-14	8	Counting Sand / *God knows what he's doing*
Exodus 20:7	10	The Job Briefing / *Honouring God's name*
Numbers 21:4-9	12	The Sheep Stuffer's Sentence / *Justice*
Matthew 7:1-5	26	The Court Case / *Hypocrisy*
Matthew 12:46-50	28	Ananias, Where Are You? / *Obedience*
Matthew 21:1-9	16	A Likely Story / *God of the details*
Mark 2:13-17	18	Veronica's Virulent Virus / *Being saved*
Luke 2:8-20	20	It's Happened! / *Spreading the good news*
Luke 11:2	10	The Job Briefing / *Honouring God's name*
John 3:14-17	12	The Sheep Stuffer's Sentence / *Justice*
John 10:1-11	22	One Man And His Voice / *The good shepherd*
John 15:9-13	14	This Thing Called Love / *God's idea of love*
Acts 9:1-19	28	Ananias, Where Are You? / *Obedience*
Acts 17:16-34	30	Conversation Pieces / *Witnessing*
Romans 12:3-8	32	The Soap Superstar / *Help from the Holy Spirit*
1 Corinthians 12:1-11	32	The Soap Superstar / *Help from the Holy Spirit*
1 Corinthians 13:8-13	34	The Perfect Sculpture / *What will we be like in heaven?*
2 Corinthians 11:14	46	Too Good To Be True / *Recognizing the enemy*
Galatians 3:26-29; 5:22-23	24	United / *The peace of God*
Galatians 5:22-26	36	Manic Mike's Paranoia Problem / *Self-control*
Ephesians 4:1-13	32	The Soap Superstar / *Help from the Holy Spirit*
Ephesians 6:10-18	46	Too Good To Be True / *Recognizing the enemy*
1 Thessalonians 1:2-3; 4:1-18	40	To Work or Not To Work / *Preparing for Jesus' return*
1 Thessalonians 5:1-11	38	You've Been Warned! / *Jesus' return*
James 1:12-15	42	The Challenge / *Temptation*
James 2:14-18	44	The Pat Rowaneyes Show / *Belief and action*
1 Peter 4:7-11	32	The Soap Superstar / *Help from the Holy Spirit*